# Taking it to the Limit

# Taking it to the Limit

poems by
Verlena Orr

DANCING MOON PRESS
NEWPORT, OREGON

Taking it to the Limit
copyright © 2009 by Verlena Orr
**All rights reserved**

ISBN-13: 978-1-892076-66-3
Library of Congress Control Number: 2009936471
Orr, Verlena
Taking it to the Limit
1. Title; 2. Poetry


Cover art by Jon Zander
Cover design by Studio Blue West, Newport, Oregon
Book design by Carla Perry
Author photo by Mehrdad "Sasson" Larki
Printed by LazerQuick of Newport, Oregon
Manufactured in the United States of America


DANCING MOON PRESS
P.O. Box 832, Newport, OR 97365; 541-574-7708
www.dancingmoonpress.com
info@dancingmoonpress.com

$10

OCLC
635589686

**FIRST EDITION**

# Acknowledgements

*Many thanks to the editors who chose these poems for publication.*

| | |
|---|---|
| **Alchemy** | The Waiting |
| **Anemone** | Life in a Capitol City |
| **Basalt** | Elegy for Ken, My Senior Dining Companion |
| **Cache Review** | Driving Home Past Redrock |
| **Calapooya** | Tangle |
| **Calyx** | Middle Age, Missoula |
| **Chariton Review** | Letter to Philip Levine from Idaho |
| **Clackamas Literary Review** | |
| | Your Unfinished House |
| **Connections** | What I'm Talking About When I Talk About Vacuuming |
| **Fireweed** | Forget Gods and Goddesses |
| **From Here We Speak: An Anthology of Oregon Poetry** | |
| | Learning the Language from Dad |
| **Fusion West** | Saturday Night at the Singles Dance |
| **Heliotrope** | Turning Sixty: The Odometer and the Sun Roll Over Another Hundred Thousand |
| **Hubbub** | Conversation at the Blue Moon Bar |
| | Crossing Against the Light |
| | The Biographical Shape of Enchantment |
| | A Small Matter of the Golden Rule in a Posh Inner City Condo |
| **Montana Anthology** | Soaring into Something Clear in a Dark November |
| **Mr. Cogito** | The Importance of Laundry (*online*) |
| **Nerve Cowboy** | The Trust Circles |
| **Northwest Magazine – The Oregonian** | |
| | Holds |
| | Fishing with a Rodeo Writer (Rider) |
| **Oregon English Journal** | |
| | Timberline |
| | Eclipse in August |
| | Missing You in Maui |
| | The Instructor Speaks from Her Pulpit |

**Oregon English Journal (continued)**

|  | The Instructor Unlocks the Door, Turns On the Lights, and Leaves the Classroom |
|  | When One Has Lived Too Long and Written Too Little |
| **Poet & Critic** | Reverence |
|  | Alone with the Cat |
| **Pointed Circle** | Pink and Black |
| **Portland Review** | Writing Exercise |
|  | Notes Without Envelopes |
|  | After Leaving |
|  | The Gift |
| **Slow Dancer (UK)** | Living with Binomials |
| **Street Roots** | Mirror Pond |
| **Suisun Review** | Calling Billie Jean |
| **Sunrust** | The Year the Steer Escaped from the State Fair |
| **Talus & Scree** | Paintings from the End of a Marriage |
|  | Coasting to a Stop |
| **Windfall** | Broken Summer in Bend |

**Windsock Poems Anthology**

Kah-Nee-Ta Landscape

Postcard from Seville

**For Paul Zarzyski**

Straight shooter poet, mentor, friend.
With thanks for keeping me going and
climbing back on the poetry horse no matter what.

# Contents

## SECTION IV:
## HOPELESS LIAISONS

## SECTION V:
## GHOST RIDERS IN MY CORNER OF SKY

## SECTION VI:
## "GEE, AIN'T IT FUNNY HOW TIME SLIPS AWAY"

# Section 1

# A Good Time Was Had By All

# Coasting to a Stop

Driving a black thread to the Pacific,
the alternate route unravels
a twisted marriage.  At fifty, I follow
you in your blue Chevy
ready for a tattoo,
the permanent butterfly.

Living lean, I have left
the legal system—whore of credit
cards, slut of dinner parties.
As I travel, his old wire that held me
stiff as a bad puppet, finally fails.

Tonight you and I shall speak
of money—we will have none.
Roses—someone will send some.
We will close our museums, lie together.

Double clutched and shifting down—
Our last stop—The Whaler
You:  Across from me
Talk:  Small with a shining underbelly
Eyes:  Green Echoes
Hands:  On the Table    Open.

# Your Unfinished House

*for John Pool*


A new broom, the remainder of your old dream,
leans between bare studs, a naked narrow bed.
Porcelain bone of the unconnected claw-foot guards
the corner window, the view — twisted berry and pine.

Someone has left a mattress,
its rose espalier a permanence climbing
over the definite edges.  Shadows will gather
later in the moon's thread as we fold
our guilt for warmth.

Now we share Oreos, breaking them
open like dark oysters, eating the filling,
as always, first.  Our votive candles hold
their own over the last webs of light,
encircle the room, make us young.

When it is dark, I will move
into your heart's fourth dream,
the flat roses will give up their scent,
blackberries turn from red to violet.

When it is dark, you will tell me
it was you who did the final sweeping.

# Living with Binomials

Subtle as night pulling over in summer,
it begins with a slip of the tongue,
then calling me by the wrong name.

What if I die? You ask that question
smiling and the joke falls of its own
weight. Scared, we blame each other

for not laughing. We make a trip for
food, but I forget what we came to buy.
You will have nothing but juice. I fall
back on peanut butter.

The cat, suddenly afraid of us, escapes
through the bathroom window and drops
into wet grass which scares him even more.

At noon, you come home to announce
you will win the Nobel Prize and that every-
thing depends on the square root of two.

You diagram Pascal's Triangle, work with
binomials and read the Bible paying attention
to only the shape of the words.

I know there is nothing I can do but love you.
In your face my face takes its cue and I am
the mirror of your courage. This bravery

begins each day taking a shower, brushing your
teeth, combing your hair, dressing and tying
your shoes. These are your acts of faith.

# Tangle

In her kitchen, three decades past wood stoves,
Mom has supper in hand—floured T-bones
fried in lard, green beans boiled with bacon rinds
since morning, spuds yanked from peace in their hills.

We have company in the living room—
a scrubbed shiny cowboy perched on the platform
rocker, turning his hat in his hands, fingers knotting,
unknotting. He is here to talk pasture with Dad,
who is still in the field baling alfalfa. Waiting,
he is obliged to visit with me.

I fumble with weather, the hailstorm that wiped out
the Wemhoff's wheat, shy away from spotted owls
and Californians. His new shirt is stiff, mother-of-pearl
buttons jailing the last of the sun, front pocket for Camels.
He relaxes into his next rodeo, Fourth of July
at Cottonwood, money and bones on a Brahma,
an eight-second life time.

This man could loan me his fishing gear,
tie leader on my line, share his angle worms
writhing in a rusty tobacco tin. I could watch him
crawl through barbed wire, move upstream.
Lonely, I would break an inch from the tangled worms,
keep it on the hook, cast until it bleached gray.

This cowboy could bring rainbows to the edge,
make me a believer of gold at the beginning and end.
I could live on the fat of this dark land
just for the joy of his hard-working hands.

# Conversation at Blue Moon Bar

Tyrone: (a bit drunkenly) "Will a whore go to a picnic?"
—Eugene O'Neil, *A Moon for the Misbegotten*


Invite me.  I only live
through an occasional window.

Everything will change with
the stained glass in June:

> A mask of a king crowned
> with Van Gogh stars.

> A baby curled in hourglass sand
> waits to be turned over.

Three months of crammed Spanish,
I learned my name is a contraction

of something red and truly beautiful
in moonlight.  Something wild in Bogotá.

Make my invitation a bottle of tequila,
its worm languishing on the bottom.

I'll bring salt and fresh limes.
I'll wear my name.

# Breaking the Fast in Mazatlan

The waiter asked me twice
if I was alone.
Twice I said yes.

But that was before
the red-footed pigeon arrived.

I told him he was handsome.
I told him he was very brave.

He ate from my plate.
Americanos screwed up
their faces and pointed.

We didn't care.
The pigeon stayed with me,
maybe for food.
I stayed out of love.

# Section II

# Where I've Been On The Way Home

# Life in a Capitol City

*after Pablo Neruda*

Under all the official titles
the stink of boiling wood.
Under all the statues
a stink of rotting salmon.
Under all elections, an aroma of trees,
a smell burning past the sunlight
in the lying sunset of this city.

The river is real.  I know that.
And the bridge connecting us.  I know that.
I am not here to see the river.
I have come to listen to clouds
boiling from concrete buildings as they dry.

Small knives turn to rain.
You chant dust, try to stop
the endless women carrying paper
the endless women carrying letters
laws in black and white.
I bring charges on all the paper

pouring over us.  There is a world
of green rivers, long distances in the jaw
of Chinook closed by the state.  It is a conspiracy
of words escaped from the order of pages and bound
volumes feeding our habit.  Men and trees lay
their smell underneath all official titles
and silence fills the valley.

# Postcard from Seville

Here, every sky is a blue glaze
fired without fog or clouds.
So certain, there is no fear.

At dusk, I hear canaries like piccolos
above the brass of traffic.  A crowd
of piccolos, but it is only one bird,
a yellow streak on the chocolate turn
of night, and I will carry this small cup of sound

when I try to tell you of Sunday at the bullring,
the counterpoint and glare of color, the rhythms
for five kills, how we clap for the last thrust.

For pictures, light in the ring is too dim.
How will you believe the turns, the poses?

So I will tell you of sky and canaries,
measured for this Sunday that moves
in me like a dance. *Adagio.*  The stun of sound
is one way to say what my skin knows.

Listen to this sky like a low flute.
It will stay and stay,
and stay.

# Calling Billie Jean

In shades of red,
our voices rainbow
a thousand miles.
Because it's so far,
we shout our poems,
believe them toll free.

We echo carmine and vermilion,
our blood magenta.
This sky melts to one red,
falling from rose to fuchsia.
Our husbands will pay.

We secure the ends
of the line.  Sister *poeta*,
our bridge arches
the long span,
holds us over
the facts in our lives.

# Certainty

"The sky settles everything..."
E. M. Forster

1. Summerfallow

October 1, 1939, my birth day.  My father made one round
of the field each day on foot behind a two-bottom plow,
pulled by his best team of horses, Molly & Star.
He set the angle and depth of the blades, turned the land
to lay fallow, rest below the snow, and wait.

2. Spring Seeding

I remember the John Deere's iron wheels, popping engine
dragging the moons of the Goble disk.  Next, harrow spikes,
then gentle curves of the springtooth making the land a fine bed
ready for the drill to portion and release seed of barley or wheat.
Waiting for it to clear up, for it to rain, gambling on no hail.

3. Summer

The months had no names. We reckoned our time before harvest,
after harvest.  During harvest it was harvest.  Then, tallying up
yield, figuring in money docked for Canadian thistle, wild oats,
mustard, too much sun or rain.  Everything was a gamble—
weather, fear of accident or illness, vagaries of supply and
demand.  It took keen savvy, stubborn will, and luck.  Always
hovering—my parents' memory of The Great Depression.

4. Fall

Camas Prairie's rhythms in my veins, I'm content this languid
afternoon.  The crop is in, the yield high, the price good.  It's
not too hot.  It's 1957, enough profit to pay cash for that Blue
Heron Chrysler that lasted fifteen years.

# Prying Open My City's Day on the Ides of March

Ten to six when the birds usually begin, but not today.
Today is broken. It's still raining. A tubercular car starts,
chokes to take hold, hacks as it warms to pull away.
A semi growls under my window, guns its motor
to take-off speed to make the green light.

Finally, one silly bird begins and a few goofy
ones join in. Homesick, I hallucinate meadowlarks
on Camas Prairie. Joggers' chatter drowns out my birds,
real or imagined, and what passes for light breaks
as Portland begins its morning rituals. Waste management
arrives, opens its jaws, hoists our refuse with a hydraulic
whine, carries off all we want out of our lives, hauls it
east for burial in the desert's mass grave.

The birds take vows of silence, and I give up, tune in the daily
freeway carnage and alternating songs—"I'm all out of love,"
"When a man loves a woman." I want things back the way
they were with a foot of new snow in Missoula, when my steps
were the first to break trail. The hard-working stars went
back to bed, and the day arrived clear, cold and delicious.

# Mirror Pond in Bend

A young couple hold hands, drift
the grassy edge of Mirror Pond.
Geese that live here have mated for life.

This first day of this summer calls up an old winter
when my favorite bar went broke.  Now, memory
opens the doors of the finest places with no cover:

Metolious Headwaters, the Deschutes, Paulina Lake,
its obsidian edge.  Will they close, give up in despair,
move to a better location?

Today, I walk the pond's circle,
memorize its new reflections—
wild blonde roses, pale azure iris,

paired geese giggling
as I move closer
to their happiness.

# Timberline

Snow clots on the frozen veins
of pine as they lean from dark
green to black.
A mountain is rumored here.

Lodge pole pine spikes
the smothering sky.
Snow piles up.
Fog pulses in with obscure warnings.

I want out of here.
Shall I start climbing?
Shall I risk tripping up
on my illusions?

I'm sure I saw an exit years ago.

I'm breaking track downhill now,
making my way back to what's left.
Snow tries to blind me,

but I was born knowing the land's
Braille, find my way on foot.

# Crossing Against the Light

December, lights flicker, lie
about everything.  Signals turn red,
and I cross anyway.

Stars give up, settle in dead or dormant
branches flanking a chain store.

Noon, someone flips a switch,
and imposter stars show up blinking.
Echolalic loudspeakers vie for an audience.

> Silent Night
> Silent Night
>
> Holy Night
> Holy Night

Calm?  Bright?  Gray is the truth.
Faithful, I'm stone deaf, adore myself.

Another friend gone.  I hear the elegiac
sigh of the sky making room for him.

Mother, please embroider some new stars
for me.  Stitch them in violet, lower them
at the speed of light on a silver-blue
crocheted chain.  I want them for Christmas.
Send them now.  I seem to need them today.

# My Last Impression of Lava Butte

I paint this hill from the top
with a broad A the color of dried blood.
There is no perspective to show the road
as it twists, swirls in on itself, ends at the rim
of the crater. I come to record extinct
fire the hill marks like a grave. Strokes of oil
show the patina of black rock at the base.
Color is not distinct from this height.

I wash the sky, brush in yellow streaks
so heavy all colors run, die in dull mud.
The hill swallows the sky, collapses in a barren hole
filled with boulders, cast off black pine branches.
Strangers drawn there ascend in their campers
lining up on the wrong side. There are no guardrails.

I look for a mapmaker to etch names of rocks
and birds, trace the flow of lava and rivers.
I paint with a feather I found in an unexpected place,
stroke the sun splintering the blue of scrub jays, mute
rust of the caldera no one descends.

Lines of my sweat dry in a thin veneer, crack
with age. Cascades to the west, blue with distance,
frame webs of smoke from the mill in Bend. This blister
hill is dead. Still, yellow pine and juniper root in ash
as this deep hollow sucks rain to the core,
festers to blow stone more durable than bone.

# Kah-Nee-Ta Landscape

Night, the still black rock,
burns after sundown.
The day's heat in my throat,
I cut a clear trail
with tumbleweed knives.

Sage moves in on a vein of green wind.
The knots, my hands, untie,
turn to red centers in Queen Anne's lace.
My arms are stalks of fireweed.

There is another way to kill:
break stems of wild flowers.
Death to larkspur and Indian paintbrush.
Daughters admire lupine in a jelly jar.

If I say sky is one bridge,
the span of color in these hills
like a new river through dried blood,
the lupine will root.

But you are here in one cool cry
of the coyote and it is night,
nothing more.

# Missing You in Maui

*for John Morrison*

Up to my neck and alone tonight
in Jacuzzi swirl, the Republicans
retired hours ago to count their money.
The hot water is all mine.

Poolside umbrellas, trussed
like misbehaved angels, serve
as lifeguards, turn in as sleeping Geishas,
hair in topknot, serene as ti plant protectors.

Dawn, angels and Geishas will go back
to their shading day job.  If you were here,
we wouldn't talk literature.  We'd lean back
in our lawn chairs, eyes closed, silent.

I would sport my trifocal sunglasses.
Your mouth would wear its Mona Lisa smile,
and we would eavesdrop the whole day,
doing our best to look harmless.

# Section III

# My Muse Smokes Camel Straights

# Learning the Language from Dad

It begins under the John Deere.
At first it sounds like thunder
over by Cottonwood, twenty miles west.

But it is the incantation
of the slipping crescent wrench,
that sacred oath of B's like bells,
S's that steam in a long train
coupled with "ings" that ricochet
in the walls of the abandoned granary,
echo the canyon
clear down to Seven Mile Grade.

Wings drumming, pigeons fall
from the hay mow
then rise like death.
The sow, gasping, lifts her snout
from the morning slop.
Whining, Old Jack runs under
the milk house where cream
goes sour in the separator.

Silver, the new palomino only Dad can ride,
snorts and lays his ears back, ready to throw
any rider, and last, the loose two-by-four
in the bunkhouse falls and crashes
like the end of a long celebration.

# Notes Without Envelopes

Dear Sister

I bought the get-well cards
you wanted sent for your recovery,
signed them love twenty-one times in America,
put them all in a blue letter box in London,
hoping they would go on separate planes.

Dear Dad

I will likely die before you
decide where your land makes you
most loved.  I hope to go in a polka.
Last week, I waltzed with a man, he could not
move his feet in a box-step, hold his back
straight, his left arm stiff.  I tried to lead.

Dear Young Man at the 76 Union Station

I list from the wheel
reasons to do without you.
Lingering does not please me
without color and detail.
I sign for the weather.
It is a friendly divorce.
You return my keys, I give
your pen back.  The charge card
is mine, the clipboard yours.
We both have a copy.
Once I told you not to fool

with the windows.  You said
you didn't want
to fool with them anyway.
Something I've always suspected.

Dear Margaret

Thanks for the invite
to see your gallstones.
In your window they will soak up winter.
I, too, save bits of rock—none
of my own growing.

To the Pope in the Dream

I don't remember the punch line
of your joke.  It was, you said,
fine to tell everyone how much fun you were,
that your friends call you Johnnie,
your mother calls you Honey,
and I can call you brother.

# Writing Exercise

Write about what is inside of you.
Have an animal or place or thing
speak for your feelings.
    There's a .22 bullet inside of me.

Is the bullet like an animal?
    It's fast and strong,
    short, like my sister, Helen.

Is it happy or sad?  Does it sing
or dance?  Could it remind you of a rainbow?
    It did sing through my lung,
    and danced near my heart.
    It yelled, "I love you"
    when it ricocheted.

Do you have something else inside of you?
What about a place?
    There's a canyon carved
    by erosion.  It's filling with water.

Are there birds living there?
    Black and white magpies.

What are they doing?
    Circling.

What do they sound like?
    My mother.

Try putting a foreign country inside of you.
   Hawaii, where my friend is dying,
   addicted to sun, swimming in gin,
   and waiting, waiting
   for Helen.

# Forget God and Goddesses

My muse, nameless, illiterate,
smokes Camel straights, sometimes rolls
her own.  I thought for sure she would show up
at Delphi as Erato's little sister
posing on the egg-shaped
rock there, once the navel of the universe.

It was raining.  The view
fogged in.  No written prepared
questions from me.  I had my soggy
snapshot taken with the egg.

I skipped out on the group tour of a museum,
looked for her.  There she was at a *taverna*
in downtown Olympia, hanging with George,
the jeweler, swilling Greek coffee and making plans
for an evening of ouzo, George, and a cheap gold ring.

I thought I'd seen the last of her,
but last fall she showed up again in a stranger's living
room, glued to the TV, chain smoking and rooting
for both college football teams.  Clearly driven
by the cut of their uniforms, she was shameless
about the tight ends and wide receivers, rolled
vulgarities around in her mouth, flicking them
off her tongue on every play.
Hopeless as a muse,
I've never seen in a dress, let alone
a diaphanous gown, she doesn't float
in beauty, but tromps around sleazy

dives in beat-up penny loafers,
men's Levis that fit way too tight.
She can't read.

The selfish witch steals, lies, leaves me
with her refuse—dangling bits of participles,
modifiers gone wild, homeless adjectives,
phonetic spelling, an entire book of split infinitives.

I've fooled her now though, convinced her
"fricative" is a filthy word. I've given up
on her, leave the schizy bitch with that word hissing
through the few remaining teeth in her nasty mouth.

# The Instructor Speaks from Her Pulpit

"Your life makes a difference here," she begins,

and rivers begin to rattle in Spanish.  Black pines
listen as innocent students stroke thighs,
rub shoulders with death.

"This is a safe place," she intones,

and the men date their mothers,
cigarettes crawl off the kitchen table, and love
affairs begin with bananas and tomatoes.

"Give me a concrete place to stand," she orders,

as they endure earthquakes of the heart, name
the exact location, ride the cold north wind,
assassins of fear, named, on the edge
describing the geology there.

"Lower your standards," she insists.

Everyone quits showing up in little black
dresses and Rolex watches, ditch gold chains
and diamond tennis bracelets.  They begin to show
off their scars, pick scabs and open old wounds—
blood flowing on through their endless Sundays.
Emily unties the apron strings.

"Read this poem as a dull child would perceive it."

30

Then all the moons become half-eaten cookies, a break
in the cloud cover, and they prance and wave red flags,
imitate voices of peacocks. Eyes shut, they leap to savor
and nurse from someone's missing ginger jar.

"What is this poem about?" she asks, then tries to answer
the question. Theft? Or maybe Loss? I don't know.
Mumbling to herself, she returns to her stone tablet,
its first command, "Show, don't tell."

# The Instructor Unlocks the Door, Turns on the Lights, and Leaves the Classroom

Poems were sired here in silver thaw ice,
clear and brittle, before Chinook Winds
arrived, opened the windows for native tongues
to ricochet through the old graveyards of beating hearts.

Maudlin siren verses ditched and ignored, everyone held hands,
craned their necks to see the new moons. Poisonous violet
larkspur showed up in star gardens where spiders lived unafraid
in their endless, exquisite webs.

Pain was served in tiny bone china cups—anapests and trochees
seemed vulgar—as all left the safe iambic drone, deadly exact
rhyme, and took up their arrhythmic lives, turned them loose to
stampede and trample endangered wild flowers.

Birdbills and shooting stars hung on. Trillium came back early.
Elusive beargrass bloomed in inappropriate places.
This instructor's sage ghost gave way.

Everyone coiled to strike blindly like rattlesnakes in August,
shedding their old skins. New voices came out of hiding,
sunned their tender scales on granite, and I turned in my key,
left the lights on, younger than I think I've ever been.

# Fishing with a Rodeo Writer

Yesterday he was an eight-second ride
on a wild horse.  Today he loans me
his leather belt, gives me the last
tobacco tin of worms.  We must crawl
through barbed wire to get downstream,
fish opposite edges.

He holds the rod like reins on a bridle,
lets it lie in his palm, eases line through
riffles surfacing in my veins as his belt turns
on my waist, and I cast towards center.

He ties leader to my hook with a knot
of wisdom that could hold a marriage together.
Scabs on his knuckles break when he makes
the delicate twist and his fingers pull me
into dark water along the bottom rock.

# When One Has Lived Too Long
# and Written Too Little

*"Oh! Poetry is like farming —*
*a lot of hard work and there's no money in it."*
Karel Wemhoff, Idaho Farm Wife

Of course, it is harrowing.

Endless plowing in circles and the sky settles everything
with its tantrums of hail,
hoarding rain or unleashing it with
wind that always gets its own way.

Every year a gamble
on high yield and a good price.

In most years, there is the September trip to the bank
after harvest to pay back and borrow more.

No fringe benefits
No gold watch

telling time in the golden years.

Only a water glass of cheap whiskey

with an hour spent in the recliner
held together with duct tape.

Stove up with arthritis, body worn threadbare,
knuckles white, joints swollen,

then crawling back on the John Deere tractor,
making round after round until the heart stops.

# Reverence

By Christ, I never thought
it would happen, but here I am
standing in my mother's kitchen
with an epiphany while frying chicken.
I ponder gravely while turning
breasts and thighs
trying to fork slippery hearts.

In one turn of a breast,
I know Mom will never bang the iron
on Dad's overalls again, and Dad
climbed on his John Deere
the last time three years ago.
Have I galloped my last horse?
Afraid of a dead run,
do I have to settle up?

I once believed it would be my choice—
a glamorous pose, one hand flung above
my head, the other limp by an empty
pill bottle. I know now some sonofabitch,
someday, will jump the gun,
and I will lose.

Here the view is cottonwood and Noble fir.
Chicken spits and hisses, set on burning
in the cast iron skillet. In the long line
of women, their reverence for eggplant and
artichokes, I take my place, circle the arena
riding full bore and hell bent for leather.

# Letter to Philip Levine from Idaho

We share no childhood landscape
but our wrenching of wildflowers
from their beds, futile transplanting
for beauty we wanted close by.

You, with your wild iris in a Detroit suburb,
your persistent search for "sandy loam."
My struggle with lamb's tongues
and buttercups half the continent west.

What we shared—a stubborn tenderness—
for what we loved and killed to have near.

One early April Idaho I found the first
patch of buttercups and gave up—
gathered bits of shale and sandstone
surrounded each plant where it had rooted.

I, too, Dear Mr. Levine, still grieve over
the deaths I caused, still reluctant to leave
the world alone. I now pause, surrender, and regard
the wild gifts, all of them, here for a reason.

# Soaring into Something Clear in a Dark November

All afternoon the window stopped
the starlings, as though they had
given up as birds.  By dark,
two feathers remained bound
by blood on the glass.

Determined birds, they tried
to pass through something clear
as I wrote on the opposite side
of the pane that made us believe
there were no boundaries.

We can't stop trying
to break through —
no matter how black
November falls,
no matter what.

# Tying One On

High as kites, in our cups,
three sheets to the wind,
we weren't drinking liquor never brewed.
We weren't inebriated on dew.
We were knocking back
double lattes and poems.

We gulped language. Totally parched,
we stole from the best, pillaged, looted,
and captured every word we could get our pens on.
We pirated peignoir, stole salal, took off with
a red wheelbarrow. "Much madness is divinest
sense," was our mantra until we were reeling,
loaded to the gills, wearing silly grins.

I remember it started to rain, and we kept writing—
neither of us with sense enough to go inside.
Finally, paper soggy and limp, ink dripping into a blur,
we called it a day. Pure debauchery.
Emily would have been proud of us.

I think you drove off in the deluge. I staggered
a block, stopped to lean on a reclining wall
of a gardener's garden next to a five-foot-long
green braid of a daffodil-spent foliage. I noticed
it was topped off with an empty pint of MD 20-20
Orange Jubilee. Sobering a bit, I scrawled Jubilee
to remember the flavor, then lurched on home,
totally smashed, totally happy.

# Section IV

# Hopeless Liaisons

# The Biographical Shape of Enchantment

Mystified
            she said
I do
            to a landscape
            of dry martinis
            lavender nightgown
            matching peignoir
A desert filled with gifts
            Dansk
            Danish Modern
            Teak
Dutiful she gave her body—
            a campsite—
                        chose a name
                        for the baby
Years a vacant chain
            on a charm bracelet
            begun with a heart, a diploma
Rage piled on her body like stone
            and she fled to a canyon
            of brandy and spy novels
She gave up
                        sex and dusting
            strangers
                        asked her for money
All that was left of her
            relentless river
            repeating itself
            with extreme irregular curves

# Paintings from the End of a Marriage

Black cows and calves inked on the dull green field.
I tear days from their roots. Someone has drawn me
in this sketch. I am framed in green that argues
with the lowered sky. I dream of wild dogs chasing me
out of the picture. No one tracks me.

White eye of the larkspur.
It would be so simple, the open mouth of rage.
This single eye stares me down. It is the moon
in a violet sky. It makes me brave as I crawl
to morning.

Long-handled mirrors of the zinnias.
I see myself in the flower, an intricate center
surrounded by crude sun. I am sad. I am old.

Leaves of cottonwood teeth.
Strident as rattlesnakes, their whir and buzz
chews raw tissue of the day as it falls
from a matted sky. Gumming my time
like a leftover. Black birds fly
speaking tongues leaves know.

Brass staccato of marigolds.
My tongue cuts stone and says I must leave.
It takes little breath and my mouth makes
a perfect circle. We cannot own anything.

Volcano rising in the center of a poppy.
This is beautifully dangerous.  I see the red eye
darken to black.  It lifts me from where I crawl.

Ashy throats of wood violets.
Dry, I cannot speak.  I dream of webs.
There is time for anything fragile.

The green marble buds of a peony.
They have no fragrance.  Of what use is something
without a smell?  I could kill them with a snap.
Burgeoning with a large conceited bloom,
I would know nothing if I were blind.

The night sky crawls with stars.
Dead night covers me.
Stars, those blinking maggots, feed.

# The Trust Circles

The nurses say this is good for us —
standing in a circle on a mattress
surrounded by padded walls.
The nurses want one person to stand in the middle.
The nurses want everyone to jump up and down.
The nurses want the patient in the middle to fall
backward into waiting patient arms that will break the fall.
The nurses call this "learning to trust."

We are numb with rage, deadened with Thorazine.
None of us can reach out in time
to catch anyone. We have dropped the fly ball of our lives.
Paranoid, I refuse to play, and for that, I'm banished to sit
in the corner on the bare floor. I am ordered to silence
like death — imminent, grim.

I return to fundamentals,
the mustard seed remainder of faith
I put in imaginary hitchhikers,
chain letters to lovers who never were lovers.
How can I believe in my comrades — apostle teenagers
threatening suicide, fondly calling each other
mother fuckers
or that ultimate endearment — fuck face.
There are the alcoholic disciples who tell great filthy jokes
until withdrawal sets in, breaks their spirits.

We all have our silly notions of heaven and hell.
We have lived life everlasting
that has gone on far too long.

We know Jesus put in a helluva day at Calvary,
but we aren't grateful for his effort on our behalf.
We don't want to sit around any dreary, sterile place
even if it is with Jesus.  I don't want to be born again.
That first entry I had with high forceps was enough.
I arrived looking like a beaten prizefighter
still standing in the ring, refusing to take a fall.

And speaking of the Almighty Joke Teller,
where is his so-called only begotten son?
Where is Jesus, that prime union organizer
of rabble, scum, sick, afflicted, and the lame and halt?
He is not in this circle or sitting by me in the corner.
I believe he has taken a walk in his garden
while we are in the locked ward jumping and falling
in a padded room with only one exit.
Jesus must be leaning on that rock at Gethsemane
rolling or casting his eyes toward heaven
as if he is still the answer to every damn question.

# The Year the Steer Escaped from the State Fair

It was all in the paper,
the escape, the police,
the boy running after his steer,
who left unjudged by the officials.

Castrated, dehorned, he crossed
the tracks, missed the train
and thirty-five pedestrians.
He trampled thousands of dahlias
and marigolds, knocked down
hanging planters, spilling fuchsias
on cement porches before he came

to the Willamette, did a perfect
half-gainer from the bank, swam
to the center island.  By the time
the pursuit canoes launched,
he was in the next county.
They brought out the dogs and helicopters.
On the golf course, the steer scattered
three allergists and two surgeons,
made it to the woods.

After four days, they penned the dogs
and grounded the planes.  No tracks
sighted, the paper said.

I like to believe the steer headed
south for Nevada's high grass, dry weather.
Some place where there is no boy to wash
him with soap, blow dry his hair, fuzz
his tail in curls and feed him triple
portions of wheat.  I like to think
he turned his marbled fat to muscle,
muscle for swimming
muscle for running
the elusive muscle that left town.

# What I'm Talking About When I Talk About Vacuuming

I'm talking 1961.
I'm talking Chicago, his law school,
my banging out a living on a manual Royal Standard
fending off a lecher boss.
I'm talking using the broom on the oval rag rug,
saving up $29.95 for a Sears Canister.

I'm talking beaten down
by the coal soot, its daily grime piling up
on the window sills, moving down the hall
easier than washing the walls.
I'm talking east coast student wives clucking
their disgust, all experts on removing cinders
from their eyes.

I'm talking husband.
Setting the vacuum in the middle
of the living room to hint that I use it.
I stepped over it, made my way
to the couch, rotgut brandy
and Ian Fleming's 007, their welcome embrace.

I'm talking Oregon, 1963.  Clean.
The relations moving in.  His.
My frenzied vacuuming,
making them lift their feet, move out
of my armchairs.  Cleaning house.  Hopeless.

I'm walking now with a Red Dust Devil,
prancing my three rooms. Ferrari Vacuum—
a lover's gift. It's delicate nozzle nuzzling
all the corners, filling that fertile void
with what is usually found there.

# Saturday Night at the Singles Dance

The high thin vocalist delivers lyrics
like instructions, makes the blues sound
strangely like a weather report.
The band learned its last new song
the year I was born, and the reason
I remember my name is that it is stuck
on my chest with a cheery salutation.
No one can pronounce it.
Myopic men breathe on my neck,
their eyes inches from my left breast,
try to sound it out.

My friend froze in her chair twenty minutes ago,
her eyes glazed after her first dance.
Now it is my turn with her partner, a classical
composer who works as a landscape gardener,
who dances in a step that makes my calves ache.
He interrupts his resume with wet kisses
on my cheek, and for the first kiss,
I am grateful.
I am grateful when the pain reaches my thighs.
I am grateful for Stardust and Deep Purple.

We paid for this dance, left the dishes, to be
on time, arrive at the same moment
as whoever we look for.  We knew we could not
not be there.  We knew we could not
turn down a dance.
We are beginning now to sound out names.

# Holds

*dedicated to Don Hill*

Pinning you on the floor
I wrestled you down to,
you laughed and asked
for more than I could give you.

Much younger, dumb, together
we stole the loose change
of marriage.  I held you,
made you real, tried to take
you through years that rolled
on my thighs,

the thick days where you
threw yourself with all
your weight to keep me flat
in the haze of your blue eyes
I learned to hate my arms pinned,
the ache of the last bend
across the small of my back.

# Pink and Black

I coil, a black polyester knot in the booth,
listen to forty years of welding triumphs
and his haunting failure —
running the outside lane in the all-state relay,
finishing last at the meet of his lifetime.

He wants to remember 1953 — drive-in movies
when we kissed ourselves silly,
gasping like fish. Eager, scared, we didn't talk
or go below my necklace.
Now, I am eating lemon meringue pie

while he welds years, mask down, blind in a flare
of arcs beading seams like old scars.
Scrubbed and polished, he is all decked out
in shocking pink socks, pastel rose shirt and pants.
He talks into me, an intense dazzle.

Beyond the spitting neon of Quality Pie, he grasps
my shoulders as he would a tractor wheel,
steers me to my proper place away from the curb.
Rage, a sudden fluorescence,
sears through my years

of polite listening, feigned interest,
cheerful chatting. This man would make love
like putting a quarter horse through
her paces — a knee here, the strong pressure
from a thigh, touch of heel to flank,

tight calves on belly, his mobile phone hooked on
an engraved belt buckle.  His leaving embrace—
a "break-a-rib-cause-I-love-you"
"squeezing," as my mom would say, "all the life
out of me," my gasp and choke taken for excitement.

# Sorting Through Sister

The camera gentles
fifty years of baking
in the sun and tanning booths,
that dazzling grin, all teeth,
the pose she took
in high school still in place.
Last year, she says,
was the worst—
signing up for Medicare.

Orphaned now,
we divide belongings.
Grandma's quilts mound
on her side of the living room
like new graves.  She needs
twenty white sheets, bleached
and line dried, used
Christmas wrappings.
Sedan, Rampage, pickup—
all the old Dodges are hers.

We maneuver the kitchen.
I take the white Corelle dishes
rimmed with blue stars
matching salt and pepper.
She needs all
small appliances, aluminum
cookware—three sets,
cheap green water glasses.

Twice this year for funerals,
we have chosen coffins and songs.
Grudgingly, she let me put
a new red bandana
in Dad's back pocket,
bury Mom with a strand of pearls.
Sorting what's left, I dump
forty years of greeting cards
on her to organize and file.

After three days, I cut my losses,
leave with a lamp,
the everyday dishes, the cedar chest
that holds my wedding dress,
my share of embroidered runners,
crocheted doilies.

No belongings left,
she has quit speaking.
I send her a cheap watch
for Christmas.  She volleys
a form letter.  I rearrange
cups and saucers, put up
a what-not shelf, work
on a pose—grim and bemused—
for close-ups.

# After Leaving

*dedicated to Don Hill*

He is young
sleeping in a common dream
of two sons and a boat.
My elbow falls on the rolls
of his belly as he breathes.
Limber, I crawl
through barbed wire
of children and dogs
to the glitter over
the next rise.

He turns and the wire
hooks the throat
of his dream as he hangs
a picture of a woman,
a large calendar.

Stale weekends linger
like smoke in a closed sky.
Summer edges in on a long line
out of season.

Love is like someone
doing a survey.
Death, the angle of vision
behind the calendar, the years
I lie still.

# Broken Summer in Bend

We flirted with a commandment to break
when he drove me in his old Ford pickup
to Dillon Falls, pulsing, plunging, echoing
the canyon walls in the crush of simple elements.

"There are no fish
in white water,"
he told me.

Broken, the river changed
its rhythm—*Vivace Con Brio*—sun splinters
hung in foam.  I believed he watched me
follow him downstream, limber,
thin in my blue dress,
legs bare in my fragile fever.

"Lichen absorbs rock,
leaves dust," he said.
"It takes a long time."

We stayed until sun thickened
and fell filled with gold, magenta,
orange and violet.

Still, always in August, shooting stars
bring back that day even as I've grown old
and broken, still believing the lonely
white feathery plumes of the beargrass
tremble and wait.

# Trying to Erase the Indelible

When I saw his name, Tom-
Tom, doubled in neon
of an all-night café,
I took it as a sign
to write down the breasts
of the young thin girl I harbored.

Whatever I penciled that summer
was rooted in the body of this blonde,
brown-eyed man I clung to.  Flying high,
I doused Guerlain perfume on my thighs,
called him by scent.

I stood at crosswalks, believed
I would see him on the other side
waiting for me.  Some nights,
my tongue remembered that satin
valley resting between his collarbone
and neck and the Palouse swale
of his shoulders.  My breasts, dark
puddings, reached up to be held.

My umber body moved like wind's
muscle in ripe wheat, soon to be cut,
turned to stubble, plowed under
year after year.  Basalt boulders still surface
each spring, gathered and hauled off
on a stone boat every cruel April.

# The Importance of Laundry

You thought you were high
on his short list of possibilities,
happily babbled to him about plans,
discovered you were an errand
on his list—below laundry.

Well, of course, you started to sob,
sank to a new low, suggested a Laundromat
date where you could swill coffee, chain smoke,
listen to the rhythmic rub, whir and spin of machines.
"I'm keeping a low profile,"
he harrumphed, turning you down.

So there you were, left with your own
laundry and no setting for normal.
You are either permanently pressed,
or delicate. Your load imbalanced.
No gentle hand-washing for you
carefully smoothed flat to dry.

Look Honey, you've had all the starch
scrubbed out of you. Scorched, shrunk,
you are left limp, lobbed like a Cruise Missile
landing in his Goodwill clothes pile. Pitiful, poor
dear! You only needed to be fluffed with no heat.

# Section V

# Ghost Riders In My Corner of Sky

# The Waiting

Goldfish here, like all the people, float
then drift down as air in this dayroom weighs
heavily.  Old men sleep day and night,
their mouths open in continual awe.

Supper, the younger old slowly lift
banana pudding from dish to tongue,
while an old woman tied in her chair
constantly whispers the same question.

Mom's paralyzed right hand, a claw on her lap,
points the way home.  The Christmas tree carries
gingerbread men to a grave, and the picture window,
pasted with grace notes of paper doily snowflakes

and crowned with honeycomb tissue bells, takes us
to the last stand of cottonwood, and further
near Hell's Canyon.  This window, the clear shell
we all move toward, is certain as the drone

of the old woman's question, faded faces—
poinsettias never watered, the final white sigh
of the cottonwoods.

# Driving Home Past Red Rock

*for Wayne James*

The old woman on the back seat is dead.
Driving her home to be buried,
the son ties the bow at the neck
of her gown, wraps her in a flannel blanket.
One slipper off, her red hair gone
to white, her eyes a dull blue glare.

The black glaze of this winter night's sky
is thin as porcelain.  Stars gnaw at the edge,
and winter wheat freezes in the dark fields.
Snow leans on the land like a handshake
good as a man's word.

He wonders why she had only
one child and feels the weight
of her slowing the car.  Her vision fixes
on the back window where the exhausted moon
rises, spreads scant light on the narrow gravel
road between Red Rock and Milt Springs.

Beside this road, a solitary house throws
a thin vein of shadow toward its barn
where a combine rusts
and loose boards shift in the wind.

He tries to decide on her dress, flowers,
her wedding band, music.  Her favorite hymn
sings in the pitch of the engine.  He thinks
she is breathing, calls to her, remembers

the window is open.  He listens to her stammer
over the radio, the crawl of the motor,
the monotone of the car.

Beside the road in sagging wire,
a fence drones the miles, echoes electric
line above.  The wires move in short breaths,
as his drive cuts Camas Prairie through small
wheat towns—Culdesac at the bottom
of the canyon he must climb.

Taking the turns with his lights on high beam,
his mother sags in a permanent curve.  Arms tense,
he twists up Winchester Grade.  The skin on his face
strung tight as new fence as he swerves toward
morning and the old moon dimming.

# Alone with the Cat

If I could begin again, unashamed, I would describe this
velvet picture in my old room.  Swans have floated there
for years.  I would free the embroidered deer,
paint that white mansion to match the turquoise lake
where faded green willows close in.
I would walk the shore and all colors would return.

I would take credit for the paint-by-number stallion
rearing on a cliff, moonlight oddly streaking his flanks
where I had strayed into a wrong number.
I would remember I was seventeen,
unable to draw a pretty face for a matchbook art school.

Now, I am alone with the last stray cat.  Dad is
somewhere in heaven on his tractor.
Mom has hollered she has gone next door.
I know, then, death could be easy as pulling the light
cord, and we will continue to plow or visit.
We will speed needlessly
and make corners in a trance.  The cat yawns,
and in that exposure of teeth and tongue,
I know I will always listen for the click as the doorknob
turns, the rustle of grocery sacks, the scuff-scuff of old
feet quietly going about their business.

# A Small Matter of the Golden Rule in a Posh Inner City Condo

I always thought of him when I took a notion
to vacuum at midnight, and I didn't
because he was asleep below.
I thought of him sometimes when I banged
the ice tray just before dawn, and figured
he was used to me by now.

One late morning last November, I heard him.
I scuffed down the stairs through a light drizzle,
reluctant Samaritan, sulking brother's keeper,
found him standing in his doorway, unsteady
trying to call back the drugstore delivery.
He was stooped, trembling, precarious
and pale as a Lladro porcelain.
I yelled the messenger back.
Mr. Norville, intent on living, reached
for his potions, said nothing.

Yesterday, stiff-limbed, stumbling downstairs
dragging my aftermath of Christmas, to get the mail,
I saw his door flung wide open
filled with a hawk-faced woman
giving orders to workmen.
I forgot hope of good mail.
I had to ask.  Turned and climbed
back up my stairs slowly.  Jolted.  Pulled the thin skin
of my door shut then swiftly and deftly set the dead bolt.

# The Gift

The sound crawls through my sleep
until I unravel like surf, then
remember it's the anniversary
of your death, and your howling
cat, now mine, brings me to morning.
I reel to the living room
where Precious Gift lies spent
on the bare floor, head on his paws.
We hold a blank numb gaze,
remember to breathe, sigh in unison.

We have almost given up
on your cough from another room,
that little song you hummed
while you turned the coffee grinder,
the strip tease you did undressing—
its grand finale, flipping your bikini
shorts from your right big toe over
your shoulder, catching them with your left
hand behind your back.  I still think
I may find you again buck-naked on the couch
a rose between your teeth.

Today, I'll drive to your Pacific,
make it mine, inexhaustible
as the cat's eyes.  There will be rain,
blurred emotion, waves sighing on
that tender scar where land meets sea.
Tonight I will come home.  Precious
will stagger to me from sleep, blinking
against the light—the only cat I've ever had
who will come when called.

# Lyric Looking for the Melody

*for Bruce Latimer*

The gold wash of sun in your hair
shines when I say goodbye,
echoes in your twin's natural curls.

Your brother plucks the pure melody
he wrote last night on the guitar
he built for you last Christmas.

Friends play your music,
keep the beat going.
The twins keep time, dance,
point to your picture.

Melody still clings.
I cannot speak.  I know the moon
will keep coming back,

and black pines will weep.
Trees do that sometimes.
Creeks beginning in the Bitterroots
make a run for it.

Years ago, I passed through
Wisdom, Montana, when you lived
near Paradise, watched for fires.

You have climbed beyond
the highest lookout tower,
and the universe pauses
as it opens its door for you —

and here you are — that brilliant maverick star
lighting the trail to morning as the sun,
never denying a thing, arrives right on time.

# Eclipse in August

*for Brent Goeres*

Your voice lingers
in the whir and spill of grief.

Better a long needle
in a remaining vein

than this ugly shroud of clouds
threatening to break loose.

Will the sun return,
reach down to give us

a hand up this cliff
to the sky I try to remember?

Will there be stars enough
to fill the night without you?

Now it is the wolves howling
their answers

so deeply, no throat or tongue
can speak or repeat them.

# "Somebody pick up my pieces,
# I'm scattered everywhere."

—Willie Nelson

*for Brent Goeres (1953-2003)*

My wild darling,
how many times
must I begin all over?
I have nothing to wear.

Who will send me back
to my room to put on a slip
under my too-sheer dress?
Who will go to Tiffany's
to buy barrettes to tame
my disheveled hair?

No one left to fasten
my necklace, straighten my collar,
tuck in tags, and keep me from leaving
my room in a collision of color.

Dearest heart, I want you back
spoon-feeding me New York,
waiting in your room as I arrange
my hair in a sleek chignon,
slip on a little black dress,
but you're missing.

I hide my eyes behind
these mirror sunglasses,
slop around in black sweats.
I feel broken, and you're missing.
You're still missing.

# Unfinished Thank-You Note to Frank

*for Frank Ratté*

What a gift you are—
letting me believe
I'm piloting
our sad sad flight.

No better nurse Nightingale,
you trill each morning open,
coax me from my bed's valley
into the room of living.

You fling Aunt Eunice's wild mink stole
over your left shoulder, strut, turn,
hold an open pose, flirt
with your eyes in passion's custody.

Taking up where Brent left off,
you tuck in tags, roll me free
of cat hair, clear the debris spilled
down my front, wipe my mouth.
The Day lifts off.

Dusk, we chatter like small birds
talking over our day until night drops
its black curtain behind August's full moon,
and stars start falling with alarming speed.

# Elegy for Ken—
# My Senior Dining Companion

He was the first
to call me
a National Treasure,

and the only man
to say
I looked smashing.

Once, he announced
I was a kick
in the pants.

When asked one time
if he owned the mansion
near where he stood smoking,
he was puzzled.

Because you look like
a million dollars,
I told him honestly.

And this was enough.

# It Gets Worse Before It Gets Better

Nothing was the same after that night—
the refrigerator loaded with seasonings
I didn't know how to use,
a drawer filled with butcher knives
that once earned a living.  I kept everything
except the whetstone I guess I gave away.

My empty bed, a boat, headed out for open sea,
oars rowing on their own.  No one at the helm
of my queen-sized craft.  Never denying a thing,
the sun showed up every day.  I woke, opened
my good eye, took hold of the edge and threw out
all the spices.  I peeled back layers of Walla Walla
sweet onions, chopped them up like bad dreams.

If I wake again before I die, I'll gather all
those fluorescent plaques' bedtime prayer…
"If I should die before I wake…," stack their eerie glow
in a funeral pyre, and light the match.

Wide awake, I'll dance around that glorious bonfire.
Patient stars will go back to their places.  Slightly askew,
the moon will recover, but night will never be the same again.

# Section VI

"Gee, Ain't It Funny How Time Slips Away"

—Willy Nelson

# Middle Age, Missoula

Clouds have gathered in the last corner
of sky like a choir gone haywire,
growling about death, tongues intent
on starting fires, their heaven
a hell with gnashing teeth.

I go to a calmer hell — The Oxford —
its clatter of keno balls,
my losing hands steady on the blackjack
table, its singing green mat luring me
to one more game.

No flat stomachs or muscular calves here.
Air fills with grease and smoke as we brag
about beating the system.  Battered husbands
turned into indignant artists, sculpt
horned owls and horses, paint portraits
of the regulars.

Too damaged to support his children,
Arlo sells me wild horses in a box canyon
for twenty bucks, the horses dim in roiling
dust and vague yellow light painted
in the importance of sadness.

Fragile drinkers wrap both hands
around their coffee cups, hang on
to the wild horse life we all have,
loathe to go out
where September draws its knives.

# Fifty-Sixth Birthday at Ephesus

Walking in the ruins
I look at the faces.

Carved stone, open-mouthed
who seem
longing to speak.

The sun is shining.
It's October.

Silence, slight breeze,
light may have been
like this on the day
I was born

screaming, body bruised
deep blue and violet.

# Turning Sixty: The Odometer and the Sun Roll Over Another Hundred Thousand

The light refuses to hold its own.
Sun turns pale, slips out early,
comes back late.

Luckily, it forgets to take
small birds and lobelia.
Last year tough zinnias stuck
it out through November.

I can tell it's getting ready
to take off again.  My mirrors
can't keep it in mind.
Sometimes a bit of crystal
jails it, rehabilitates it
to miniature broken rainbows
broken and confused.

Our relationship cools.
Only a few shafts left.
This sun doesn't deny me,
just leaves, hopes I won't notice.

I wait for word, or a snapshot
that says it all—a postcard
from down under.  No message.

# Sixty-Nine & Pushing On

My hazel eyes remain,
right lid fallen, face in deep
decline—a woman
getting on and melting down.

Still I think of sin,
but the sky blackens
and can't remember its stars.
I've mislaid all my moons,

taken up eavesdropping, install
peepholes & deadbolts.  A stray
cat moves in.  I keep a plug-in heater
near when October shows up

for my birthday.  Daily creaking out
of bed, I limp into morning Prozac,
drink a pot of coffee, suck down
a fistful of cigarettes and try to figure
out the day of the week.  It has
come to this:

Young foreign men sweetly lie.
"You look beautiful," the Persian
cashier gushes.  My passion
flower perks up!

"You are gorgeous, honey,"
the Chinese housecleaner hisses
as he dusts me off.  "I can't hear you,"
I yell, just so he'll shout it again.

# Square Root of the Time of My Life

Sometimes my mind shoulders its baggage
and leaves.  No destination—
just goes to a Klee blue canvas.
A standard deviation that cannot be skewed.

It's a dance of calculus graduated
*cum laude*.  The Supremes show up
humming a rendition of Grace.
There's a correlation coefficient here.

Trust me.  The river rises at random.
Studies must be done to determine
significance.  Life is the control group.
The answers are not in the back of the book.

Are there any further questions?

# About the Author

Verlena Orr, twice nominated for a Pushcart, hails from north-central Idaho, one mountain west of Missoula, Montana. She was raised on a farm and attended elementary and grade school at Kamiah, Idaho, on the Nez Perce reservation. But she shifted to urban fifty years ago and resides in northwest Portland, where she has lived since 1980.

Her assorted jobs have been secretary, social worker, hired girl during harvest, and more recently, instructor at Portland Community College and teacher for the Portland Public School's Talented and Gifted Program. She recently produced a documentary, *Sky Settles Everything: The Wayne James Story*, about her rancher cousin, Wayne James who remained on his family farm in Idaho.

Verlena's poems have been published in journals throughout the country and in the United Kingdom. She has published three chapbooks – *I Dance September Naked in a Dream* (Howlet Press), *Woman Who Hears Voices* (Future Tense Press), and *One More Time from the Beginning* (Stone City Press). Her full-length collection of poems, *Break in the Cloud Cover*, was also published by Howlet Press. She holds an MFA from the University of Montana and continues to write, and participate in workshops and classes as a student.